THE YUMS

Potato's friends
like to call him 'Spud'

and most of the time
he is covered in mud

He once had a muddy splat
on top of his head

'It looks like a silly hat!'

That's what Artichoke said

Another time
some stuck on his tummy

and Spud
couldn't see his feet

Then some got stuck
on both of his arms

which Spud thought
was really neat

The funniest time
was when he sat in some dirt

which looked like
a great big bottom

He laughed so hard
that his ribcage hurt

so it's probably best
forgotten

Spud had a plan
to keep himself clean

by putting on
a macintosh

But a seagull flew by

and oh me oh my!

He still ended up
needing a wash

Some people like
their potatoes

peeled, clean
and bare

Which would make
Spud incredibly clean

but he'd rather have his
jacket to wear

Created by Mary Ingram

Read about Potato's friends...

Artichoke

www.theyums.co.uk

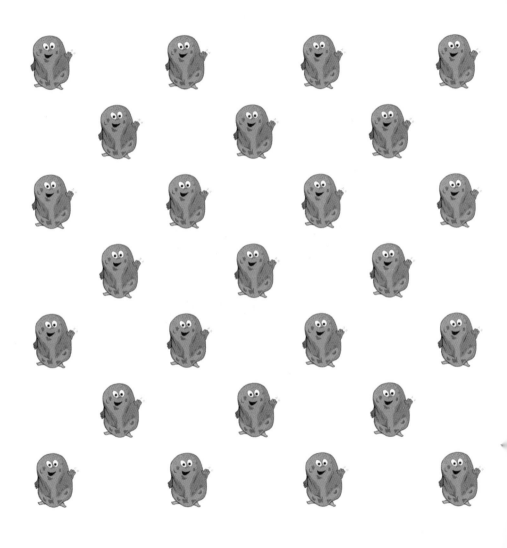

Printed in Great Britain
by Amazon

77482700R00016